A-Z of God's Promises for Me!

THANK YOU, JESUS, THAT ALL YOUR PROMISES BELONG TO ME:

NAME:
_ _ _ _ _ _ _ _ _ _ _

B IS FOR... BEST FRIEND!

God is my **best friend** and my shepherd. I always have more than enough.

PSALM 23:1

C IS FOR... CARES!

I pour out all my worries on God and leave them there, for He always tenderly cares for me.

1 PETER 5:7

D IS FOR... DELIGHT!

What delight is mine when I follows God's ways!

PSALM 1:1

E IS FOR... EVER PRESENT!

God is my refuge and strength, an **ever-present** help when I'm in trouble!

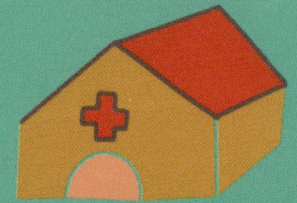

PSALM 46:1

F IS FOR... FATHER!

God is my heavenly Father. to the fatherless, You are a father. to the lonely, You give a family.

PSALM 68:5

G IS FOR...

GOOD GIFTS!

Every gift God gives me
is good and perfect.

SO GOOD

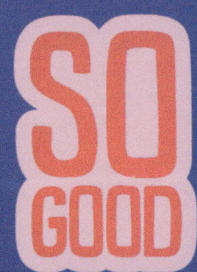

JAMES 1:17

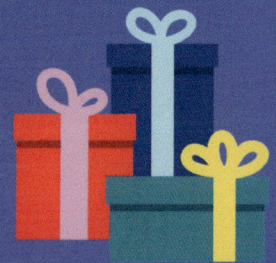

H IS FOR...

HEARS!

I know that He hears me in whatever I ask, and I know that I have obtained the requests I ask of Him.

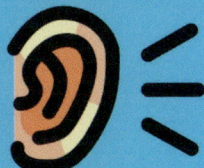 

1 JOHN 5:15

J IS FOR... JUSTICE!

God, You love seeing justice on the earth. Anywhere and everywhere I look, I find Your faithful, unfailing love!

PSALMS 33:5

K is for... KING OF KINGS!

You are king of kings, so I will bow before You. You are king of kings, every nation will one day serve You.

PSALM 72:11

L IS FOR... LOVE!

I live confident that there is nothing in the universe with the power to separate me from God's *love*.

ROMANS 8:38

O IS FOR... OVER ME!

God himself watches over me; He's always at my side to keep me safe in his presence.

PSALMS 121:5

Q IS FOR... QUENCH!

God pours out water to quench my thirst and to irrigate the parched fields.

ISAIAH 44:3

R IS FOR... RESURRECTION!

God is the Resurrection and Life Eternal. If I cling to Him in faith, I will have eternal life.

JOHN 11:25

By grace I am saved by faith. Nothing I do could ever earn this salvation, for it is a love gift from God.

EPHESIANS 2:8

T IS FOR... TRUST!

When I trust God to direct my life, I'll find He pulled it off perfectly!

PSALMS 37:5

U IS FOR...

UNFAILING LOVE!

Your **unfailing love** is better than life itself; how I love and praise You God!

FOREVER PSALMS 63:3

V IS FOR... VICTORY!

Despite all these things, overwhelming victory is mine through Christ, who loves me.

ROMANS 8:37

W IS FOR... WISDOM!

If I desire to be wise, I can ask my generous God for wisdom and He will give it!

JAMES 1:5

X IS FOR...

EXCEED!

God will do infinitely more than my greatest request or my most unbelievable dream, and will **exceed** my wildest imagination.

EPHESIANS 3:20

Y IS FOR... YES!

All of God's promises for me find their "yes" of fulfillment in Him. And as His "yes" and my "amen" ascend to God, it brings Him glory!

2 CORINTHIANS 1:20

Z IS FOR... ZION!

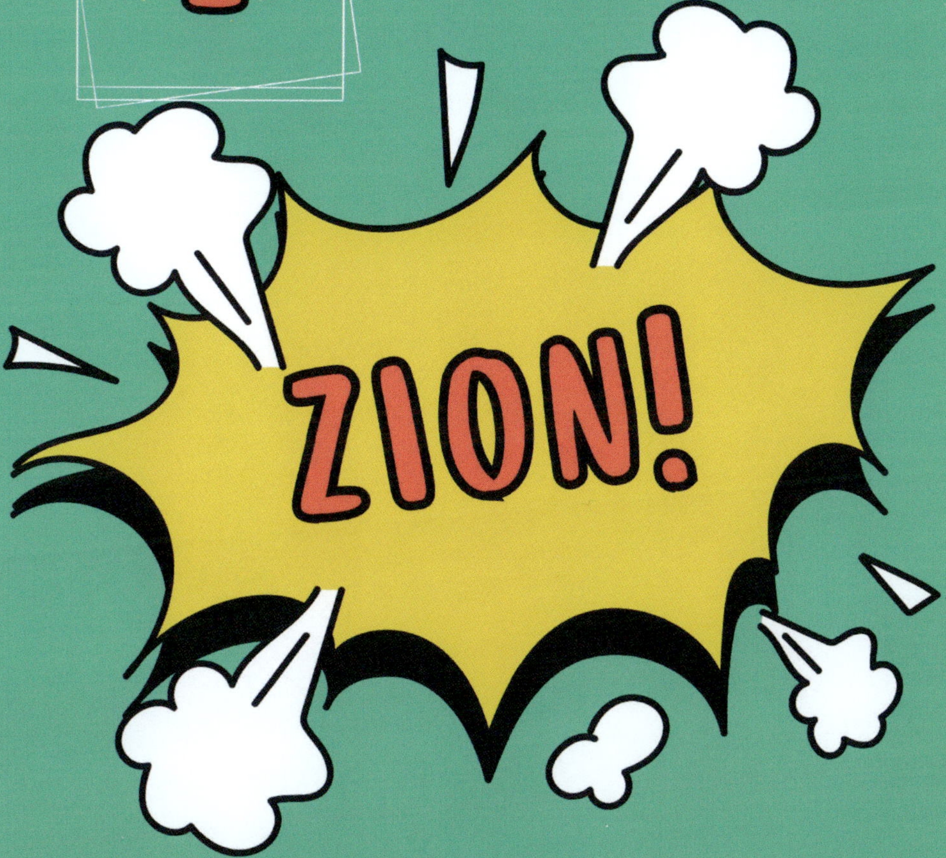

When I trust in the Lord, I am as secure as Mount Zion; I will not be shaken.

PSALMS 125:1

PRAYER

Father God, thank you that You answer my prayers. You are my best friend and I'm so grateful that You care for me. I delight in You, for You are my ever-present help when I am in need. Thank you that You are my perfect, heavenly Father and You give me good gifts. Thank you when I pray You hear me, You answer in incredible ways and You bring justice when I need it. I praise You for You are the King who is greater than every other king, your love for me is more than enough in every situation, and nothing is impossible with You. I ask You to watch over me, for your perfect peace to guard my heart, and for your Holy Spirit to quench my thirst. Thank you for your resurrection that gives me eternal life, and for your free gift of salvation. Thank you I can trust You because of your unfailing love, and because You give me victory in every situation. I ask for your wisdom to walk in your plans for me, and I'm so grateful that your plans exceed my wildest dreams! Thank you that You always say "yes" to fulfil these promises for me. Please keep me and my family as safe as Mount Zion. Amen.

Printed in Great Britain
by Amazon